Time:

Endless Moments in Prison

Author: Bobby Bostic

ISBN: 978-0-578-89957-2

Book Categories: Crime, Social Science, Criminology, Rehabilitation, Education

Table of Contents

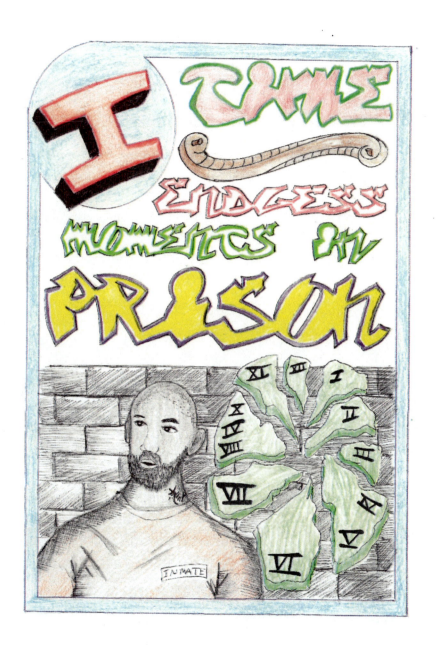

Chapter 1
Time: Endless Moments in Prison

Time is defined as being a period during which an action or condition exists or continues. It is the duration of existence. It is more of a period when something happens. Also, it's a moment, hour, day or year. In prison, time seems like it is endless. It just drags on seemingly forever. Time in prison feels like forever, especially when you were sentenced to spend forever in prison. The clock and calendar are your greatest register going through these recurring instances. When it gets super bored in here, time drags on infinity in our finite human minds. All you can do is think and stare. They say that time waits for no man, and prison shows us this each day that passes by.

We are in a time warp in prison. All we have is mental images of the world from when we last saw it, yet everything that we knew has changed. We think of time as we knew it back then, but we quickly find out that times have changed. The twenty plus years that I have been incarcerated has steadily dragged by with me sitting in a prison cell.

For those people in prison who do not occupy their time, their suffering is exacerbated because time here feels like it is all wasted to them. Being pessimistic like this makes time go by very slowly for them. We do hard time in prison, but honestly, we can get something great out of our prison time if we just apply ourselves and use our time wisely.

Of course, there are many things in prison that arc out of our control, and many unforeseen circumstances can make our time very difficult in here. No matter our condition in here, time goes on. The most difficult and slowest time in prison is when we go to solitary confinement. When a human being spends days on end, weeks, and years locked in a cell 24 hours a day, it is the slowest time we have ever experienced.

Moments just drag on even when we live in that moment. In solitary confinement, there is nothing but the walls, steel, and your thoughts. Time is passed by filling the void; reading, writing, exercising, cleaning up or anything else to occupy one's time. Yet time still seems to take forever. A half hour feels like two and a half hours. You are always just waiting on time to pass by. The entire day is based on time, but the time never seems to end. Sometimes there is so much noise and chaos going on that you cannot sleep. You have many guys in here who do the night shift. They stay up all night making noise, fishing kites (letters, notes) back and forth. Out of boredom, some prisoners flood their cells just to get some excitement (action) going or just to get the guards' attention if they feel like they are being ignored, and at other times just because they are bored. For real, it gets crazy in here.

When you get kept up all night by the mad antics of attention seeking prisoners, it really makes time stretch on forever. Then we have the day shift prisoners with their endless noise. At those times, when both sets of these prisoners have exhausted themselves, there is the deafening silence when it gets eerily quiet in here. All this drama leaves us sleep deprived. Somehow, we deal with it and move on. Nevertheless, nothing can really explain the actual human experience of time stopping on you. Time in the free world flies by pretty fast, but the same time drags on forever in prison.

In here we feel like we are in a different time zone than the free world. We feel like we lose time in here because we sure are not gaining time. Time cannot be returned to us. We can never get these years back. The emotional damage and physical trauma, the family losses, missed funerals, milestones gone by, birthdays skipped, yearly holidays, graduations, kids taking first steps, etc. all missed. Especially when you are locked in solitary confinement, no freedom of movement, no hugs, no love, cannot get any fresh air, no seeing the stars in the night sky, no sun, no cruising down the street or highways. All you hear is people hollering, screaming, crying for whatever attention they can get. One day can feel like two and a half days.

Usually in prison we are all given a cellmate. Imagine being stuck in a small room (cell) the size of a closet 24 hours with another man. Time gets more difficult then. You have to deal with the moods and habits of another human being. I use the pronoun 'he' throughout this text because prison is the same for either sexes. You are forced to listen to your cellie snore, if he does not snore you still have to move quietly and tip toe around the cell while he is asleep. When he eats, you are there, whatever he does, you are there, and there is no privacy. If dude is in a bad mood, you have to either ignore him or try to life his spirits up so that his misery will not rub off on you. Therefore, you often find yourself in prison trying to inspire others by spreading hope. If you feed into his misery, then eventually this will lead to a fight or worse in here. Throughout my twenty plus years here, I have to deal with this madness daily. It is just a part of prison.

If you do not get along with your cellmate, then months can go by without you all speaking to each other. Imagine how time goes in such a tension filled environment with you and your roommate not speaking for months, yet you are forced to be in the room with this person for at least 20 hours a day. It happens every day inside of prison due to overcrowding and cell capability requirements.

As soon as you get used to one cellmate, then he gets locked up in solitary confinement or just moved and somebody else is placed in the cell, and you have to try to adjust to another man's moods or ways. A lot of times this just doesn't work. Dealing with this type of stress is part of the endless cycle of doing time in prison.

How do you count time when it feels like there is no end to it? I know that they say life is short, but when you spend your life in prison, time does not seem short at all. Life seems longer in here with all the years that we spend with time seeming to go at half its speed. When I call home, people on the streets often tell me that there seems like there is not enough time in the day to get everything done that they need to get done. Well, I tell them that in jail, there seems like there are too many hours in one day. There is so much restriction that there is no way to break the monotony.

In time this begins to wear down some men's spirits. Without a bright future to look forward to, many men in here live in misery. This is the effect that doing dead time has on human beings.

How the Smallest Mundane Things Take on The Greatest Meaning

The smallest mundane things take on the greatest meaning in prison. In here it helps men to have something to do in order to pass time. Men break their day down in blocks of time. Everything gets done on a schedule. When someone in here wakes up, it can typically take up to 30 minutes getting themselves together: washing their face, brushing their teeth, grooming their hair, preparing a cup of coffee, etc. The little things become a big ritual in here because there is nothing else to do and no hurry to get anywhere usually. Cleaning up and being clean is especially important in here. Some prisoners become extremely obsessive about their hygiene habits. A man may spend up to an hour a day cleaning his tiny cell, which is the size of a small bedroom closet in the free world. Small things like this helps a prisoner feel in control. Since we do not have much control in here, small things take on great significance for us.

People who have braids will spend an hour or more getting their hair braided, and most do it weekly. Washing our clothes by hand takes on a great deal of time. Men take great care of the little things that they allow us to have in here. Things that are trivial in the free world are epic in prison. So much time is spent on games in here that games become serious. Competition becomes the most furious behind the walls. Games in here are not inconsequential. When people in here gamble, they put it all on the line.

Cooking meals is done with the most serious attention. Guys give their all to these meals. Just as on the streets, if someone is going to eat a meal at 7 p.m. he will start preparing the ingredients for that meal at 7 a.m. It literally takes all day to prepare some meals in here. Just having a good warm meal like this gives men in here something to look forward to later on in the day. If there is nothing else going on, at least they will have a good meal and have control over that. The smell of food becomes more intense. In here you notice things that you never have before.

The space inside your mind in prison causes you to observe everything more deeply and clearly. Memories become sharp. Nostalgia takes over. You recall and remember the most intimate details of everything. Emotions also become heightened rather they are expressed or not. We hear and see the world in a clear way that we never have before. This is why people in prison learn to appreciate even the smallest things to a great extent. Interaction with other human beings becomes significant. Family relations become monumental.

Everything in here takes on a superb meaning. Things that were once taken for granted no longer goes unappreciated. Time slows down all the while these moments in prison seem endless to us.

Chapter 2
When Do You Go Up for Parole; When Do You Get Your Answer Back

Besides being asked what are you in prison for, or when do you go home, the third most frequent asked question is, when do you go up for parole? Us prisoners get asked these same three questions almost every day from some other prisoner or someone on the streets. Simple questions, simple answers huh? Well it is a little more complicated than that. It gets even more complex because so many human lives are involved. Many men in here will never make parole. Whenever they venture into the topic of eventually going home it is spoke of with so much emotion. Although I came to prison at 16 years old and I have been here for over two decades now, my sentence required that I die in prison. It stipulated that I could never make parole within my lifetime. Fortunately, many of my cellmates and others in here can make parole, even if that date as a decade away, at least they know they're going home one day. The chance for freedom is our greatest motivation.

Long before it came to prison, parole boards across the country believed in the concept of rehabilitation and freely gave inmates parole dates. Prisoners back then only served a third or no more than half of their sentence. That all changed in the late 1980's with the war on drugs in in the 1990's with the war on crime. Many mandatory minimum laws got passed across the country. With so much recidivism taking place, prisoners were made to serve much more time on their prison sentences. Nowadays parole is a matter of privilege as opposed to a matter of right. It is up to the parole board's discretion whether they will release a prisoner or not. No one in here can be certain what decision the parole board will make and each individual case. All we can do is hope and wish for the better in here while expecting the worse.

So, when do you go up for parole man? There is a different answer from the millions of people who are in prison. The majority of us dream of freedom every day in here so of course the ultimate question is when do you go up for parole?

That is the only way that the majority of us are getting out of here. Making parole is something that we prepare for in here. What will we say to the parole board? How will we make our case? It has taken years to finally make it to this day. Everything is on the line. Before we make it to this day let me discuss the endless days leading up to the day that you finally see the parole board.

Everything that you do in prison affects your ability to make parole or not make parole. Nothing is guaranteed when it comes to the parole board if you are expecting their mercy. One way or another in prison trouble big or small will find you. There are at least 100 different rules in here that could get you a conduct violation. Each violation that you get is put in your file to be ultimately considered by the parole board. Staying out of trouble is a meaningful goal to strive for in prison, but prison presents its own set of problems.

Every day we deal with dozens of personalities and you must survive in this violent environment. Not to mention the guards in their different attitudes, personalities, dispositions, and moods. Each of these factors determine if you will get in trouble or not for even the smallest infraction. And here we say that the guards are petty for issuing small minor rule infractions. In most cases we have witnessed guards seeing other prisoners do the same thing, but they have their picks of who they do not like or will issue a rule infraction. We say that it is unfair but nevertheless this is prison and we just have to deal with it.

Certain guards will target you an issue you rule infractions for just about anything if you rub their bad side. Other guards just do this because this is just their nature. there are so many varying factors to this stuff in here. On the other hand, all of us prisoners do dumb stuff and get ourselves into trouble.

Ironically, some prisoners do not care about getting in trouble. Although actions come with consequences in here, trouble is just an extension of being in prison. When guys do things in here, they're not consistently weighing the long term or even short-term consequences of their actions. In fact, survival is our first instinct, so if trouble comes your way you have to do something about it. Surviving in prison comes with a lot of different complexities. First and foremost is to not be weak and get preyed upon by the predators in here. Guys in here will break any rule to survive, while others just break the rules simply because they do not care or feel like they do not have anything to lose anyway. Prisoners are all mixed together now regardless of how much time they are serving. I have had many cellmates that went home from the cell we shared together although my sentence required that I die in prison.

So here you have prisoners serving life without the possibility of parole in a cell with someone who only has a five-year sentence. Imagine the turn of the conversation when the person who is never going home has to talk about the streets with their cellmate who will be going home within a few months. The guy who was on his way out is talking about all of the magnificent things that he's getting ready to go out there and do, while the guy serving life without parole knows that he will never get out there to do these things. If he has a positive disposition about life in prison has not made his heart cold, then he is happy for his cellmate and gives him positive advice. If he is negative in his heart is become hardened, then he reacts negatively to his cell mate who is getting out. We are surrounded by so many negative miserable dudes in prison. It is a challenge to remain positive in here. Even the most positive prisoner has negative days in here. Others just choose to be negative because that is just who they are, or they have given up hope.

Prison has strange effects on men. Psychologically this is a heavy mental burden that some people are simply not equipped to deal with. It is not easy for any of us in here. All kinds of factors determine how someone may behave in here. Again, our behavior determines whether or not we will make parole sooner than later.

Hope is all we have in here and without hope we have nothing. So keeping hope alive is our most valuable coping tool. Making parole is how we get free. Guys in here have a ritual of crossing out days on the calendar looking forward to the coveted day that we will finally make parole. This is the day that we wait years for. The parole officers do dozens of parole hearings each day and do it as it is just another day of work for them. But for the prisoner, his entire life hangs in the balance. Getting all of our hopes, dreams, and desires, all depends on the results of our parole hearing.

When we talk to our family members, they often ask us "when will you make parole?" they ask us this question with so much love in their voice. We try to be upbeat and give them a positive answer. These people love us, and they want us to be at home just as much as we want to be there. Staff members in these places often ask the same question. After spending years working around you, they wonder when you will go home. And here day in and day out we countdown until that day. A lot of times there are certain stipulations that we have to meet before we are eligible for parole. The stipulations vary but we can be required to take certain programs as a result of our crimes. There are dozens of these classes. The main ones are Substance Abuse classes, Victims Impact classes, Anger Management classes, Restorative Justice, and Mental Health counseling.

For the prisoners who are serious about their future, these classes help them in their transition. Furthermore, it gives them something to look forward to while they're doing time. Those prisoners who are truly focused even practiced what they will tell the parole board the day that they see them. Most guys just freestyle it and say what's on their heart when they see the parole board. No matter what we say though, the parole board has everything in their file that they need to know about us to determine what their decision will be. Knowing when we go to see the parole board determines how each person functions in here. An inmate that has a chance to make parole is expected to behave accordingly. The lifers are sometimes well behaved while the short timers take their upcoming freedom for granted.

A short timer knows that the parole board eventually has to release him even if they make him complete his entire sentence. In his defiance of the system, he does not care because he will be released without being on parole with the system still having control of his life out there. The lifers wish that they had the opportunity that the short timer has. In here we know that justice is not blind, and the system is not fair. Either way we are caught up in the system and we have to deal with it.

Guys going to see the parole board have to walk a thin line and do their best to maintain a positive behavior. In a negative environment like this, it can cause you to become a target of bitter guards or hateful prisoners. It is crazy but some people want to see others stuck in here with them or just simply do not want someone else to go home. If the guard does not like you then they will issue frivolous rule infractions for any and everything which will harm your chances to make parole. Predatory prisoners will set up traps or try you by provoking you into a violent confrontation with them and that will surely deter you from getting a parole date. These are the harsh realities that we deal with in prison each day.

Meanwhile as a person serves their prison sentence, they must maintain in prison by keeping their sanity and health intact. For most people in here that merely consist of passing time. When that time comes all we can do is wonder what the parole board will do at the hearing. Who will the parole board members be? What questions will they ask us? Will they understand the reasons why we made certain decisions and internal mistakes? What were their personality be like towards us , etc. Talking about the dynamics of any given parole board is an entirely different discussion. We never know the makeup of any given parole board on any given day. What works for one inmate may have totally different results for another inmate. These people are assigned a very delicate responsibility to decide who should be released back into society as not posing a threat versus who does. No matter what is said at the parole hearing, we do not know what the answer will be until they tell us. The anticipation on waiting on what the answer will be causes the most anticipation a person has endured their entire stay in prison. Different states have different methods of letting inmates know whether or not they have made parole. Some states let the inmate know the same day while other states such as Missouri, where I am incarcerated at, the parole board typically lets you know in about 4 to 8 weeks their decision in your case.

The Dreaded:

When Do You Get Your Answer Back

After you go up to see the parole board, the hardest part is waiting on the answer. So many people are waiting on the answer with you. Until you get the answer back from the parole board you are on a constant anxiety trip. Everyone seems optimistic in here and nobody wants to sound pessimistic about your prospects of going home. So everybody gets your hopes up and says, "man they're going to give you an outdate don't worry." I guess that it is easy for them to say when it is not their life. Still, everyone keeps saying that you are going home . If you are not careful then you start to believe the hype. There is no let down greater than when you find out that you are not going home at the time that you expected to. We always tell ourselves that in order to avoid such letdowns we must just go on with the flow and let whatever happens just happen.

Although prisoners wait for many years for the answer back from the parole board, when it actually comes, we do not always have the anticipated reaction that we thought we would have. We could be caught by surprise, especially when we get that actual release date. Now it is finally time to put all of these plans into action. Freedom is finally here. If the release date is years away, then time really slows down again. Each day seemed longer until that release date finally approaches. Everything will seem different than. Life itself becomes different. Everything feels better period it is difficult to contain your happiness. Although you are still in prison, just having that date makes you feel like you are floating. People are so happy for you; it is time.

On the other hand, when your parole date gets denied and you are given a setback, it is very devastating. Depression sets in very deep in life seems to stop. It is a shock. You stay in yourself for a few days processing the bad news. You have to find something to occupy yourself and back into your prison routine until you see the parole board again which will usually be a few years. It is hard to go on, but you have no choice but to move on.

When the parole denial comes the world may have fell in on you but for everyone else around life goes on just as yesterday. And here after saddening disappointments, we all learned to keep pushing on period until that next parole date you must keep busy and maintain.

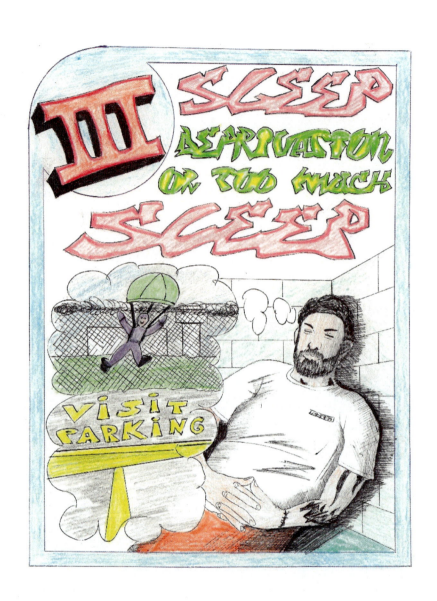

Chapter 3
Sleep Deprivation   or
Too Much Sleep

Sleep is like a drug in prison. It becomes sort of like an antidote to insanity. It is the greatest escape in prison. No where in the world will you find people who sleep more than prisoners do. A lot of men in here cannot face their failures so they sleep their time away. What greater remedy is there than to be dead to the world? That is the philosophy of men in here who do not really want to deal with a life that is showing them it's worst side continuously. Many people in the free world deal with their depression in the same way. There are hundreds of pills in a trillion-dollar Pharmaceutical industry that caters to depressed people's indication to medicate themselves and sleep all day. Some mental health doctors are quick to prescribe sleeping pills for depressed patients. Prison is one of the most depressing places in the world. The ironic thing is that prison is so depressing that you do not even need sleeping pills in order to go to sleep. And here you sleep just because there is nothing else to do.

There are many psychological components as to why people who are locked up in confinement choose to spend half or more of each day sleeping. Let me explain: 80% of all prisoners have a drug habit in the free world. Getting high or drunk out there is how they dealt with their problems. Drugs are available in prison, but not as nearly as plentiful as they were on the streets. Furthermore, drugs are not the remedy to the kind of problems that we deal with in prison. No matter how high you get you still cannot escape the fact that you are locked up.

Majority of us were sleep deprived in the free world. I slept about four hours at the most on the streets. Sleeping on the streets made us feel like we we're missing out on the action. Sleep deprivation is even more epidemic now with the rise of people who are addicted to upper drugs such as meth, etc. Those who are addicted go for days without sleeping for years on end throughout their addiction. Young people like me did not sleep that much out there because we were adrenaline junkies who always had to be off into something.

You could not hustle while you were sleeping, and we hated to miss out on the money. We were always fighting off sleep. We slept as little as possible jeopardizing our own health as well as the health of others.

It is ironic that as much as we dislike sleeping on the streets, when we were arrested the first thing that we would do is sleep. Of course, this is the result of a combination of factors. First of all, we would be so sleep deprived that we found ourselves catching up on sleep that we missed out on out there on the streets. Secondly, we would be so depressed about being in jail that we tried to sleep through it until we made bond or got out. Thirdly, we might have been suffering through a hangover or either drug withdraws, and we tried to sleep through that agony as well. After we slept for a couple of days , then we were forced to deal with our dire predicament of being in jail. Once we woke up and faced our harsh reality , it got so depressing that we went back to sleep again. This is why people automatically sleep for days when they first get arrested.

There is a small percentage of prisoners such as myself who only sleep about five or six hours a day even in prison period some of us are so goal oriented that we're awake as much as possible trying to figure out how to get out of prison and make something of our lives when we get out there. On the flip side of this are those prisoners who barely sleep because they are engaged in the prison madness that requires them to be up 20 hours a day so that they can have their hand involved in everything.

Solitary confinement takes on a deeper dimension of depression and calls for much more sleep than any human being requires. When you are confined to a cell 23 hours a day and there is nowhere to go with not much to do, the overwhelming majority of prisoners spend this time sleeping. A good percentage of people here do it with the aid of pills. Pills get abused here at an enormous rate. There is a black market for psychotropic drugs in here. Pills are purchased for getting high as well as to sleep period there are pills are so strong that they make a person sleep the entire day away. Under the influence of these powerful mental health narcotics, you muster just enough strength to get up and eat and use the bathroom and then go right back to sleep period this zombielike routine is a regular ritual for a lot of men in these cell blocks.

Years passed by in here with men living under the drug crazed influence of mental health prescribed psychotropic drugs. Each year as their bodies get used to the effects of the drugs that doctors just increase their dosage. This is the administration's main protocol for treating mentally ill inmates.

Mental health doctors in penal institutions are ill equipped to deal with their overburdened workload. For each 1000 prisoners, there are only three mental health doctors at each institution . The vast majority of prisoners are dealing with some kind of mental health issues. Being confined in a cell itself causes all kinds of mental health issues. You could take any normal functioning human being from off the streets and put them in prison and watch how their mind starts disintegrating within a few weeks. Prison can break the strongest of men. I will not cite any of the thousands of studies that confirm the mental illnesses that run rampant inside of prisons all over the world. Nevertheless, I will simply point out that even if you take a mental health doctor and confine him to a prison cell for a few years, he will be able to name a few dozen mental health maladies that he is now suffering from as a result of a few years spent in jail.

An overloaded workload and so much continuous chaos in these cellblocks spells a recipe for disaster for mental health doctors treating patients in prison. Your patient will exhibit so many varying symptoms that your years in school has never prepared you for. Just like the prisoners themselves, this places the mental health doctor between a rock and a hard place. He wants to treat these patients with the proper care, but he is constrained by security mechanisms within the system reinforced by dozens of rules of what tools he can use to help the prisoners. The doctors are limited in how much time they spend with each inmate. He has hundreds of patients under his care, so what is he to do? Men come to his office complaining of symptoms of extreme depression and his remedy for them is narcotic level psychotropic drugs that will calm him down and make him sleep to allegedly keep them out of trouble.

Ironically, these drugs often have the opposite effect, and these men end up in even more trouble. At nurse medication time you see dozens of inmates in each housing unit lining up faithfully three times a day to take these strong powerful drugs that are supposed to keep them calm and mellow. These pills are used to support these men's constant habit of sleeping. Once while in solitary confinement a prisoner in an adjoining cell gave me his pill to use and this was my first and last time using one of these pills. I slept for two days and was barely able to get up and eat my meals. I know the effect of these pills firsthand and the effect of them was stronger than the drugs that I used on the streets. In short, these pills help prisoners sleep away years of their time but also have some of them walking around like zombies. People lose a sense of themselves. Men lose sense of time under the influence of these pills. I have never been in the habit of taking these pills because I never have been able to sleep endlessly in prison. Even during long bouts of serious boredom when I wish I could sleep my time away, my mind refuses to cooperate, and my body is too energetic to be sleeping all day. I am forever active.

I am not a psychologist, but after doing over 20 years in prison I have witnessed firsthand that these psychological pills do more harm to prisoners than they do to help them. Also, there is a major percentage of people in prison, as well as immigration detention centers, who use natural methods of sleeping. In their deep state of depression, they just shut down their minds and drift off to sleep. Out of boredom they have nothing to do in the midst of their depression, so they go to sleep. What else is there to do? That is their response when people ask them why they sleep so much. Many correctional officers notice that a lot of prisoners are asleep most of the time when they walk by to look in their cells at count time or to observe them.

You may ask what is the mental reason behind this? I've attempted to explain this thus far in this chapter. Going into a deeper depth of this phenomenon I must give you a better picture of the dark clouds of depression that blanket men stuck in prison.

Under the Cover

If you ever visit a jail, dorm, or prison block, you will notice that a lot of men have their head under the cover with their eyes closed. Why? This is where a lot of our thinking is done. Under the blanket it is dark and that reflects the state of many men's lives inside of prison. It is even more difficult to explain the extreme levels of depression that we deal with in prison. It is depression upon depression for various reasons. There are so many factors involved. First and foremost is the loss of freedom. The second is being away from our family members. Third, we have no control over our movements or placements within the prison. The list is endless of all the reasons that a person can be depressed in prison. Everyday appeals get denied, family members die, wives divorce us, girlfriends leave us, we find ourselves with no funds to purchase everyday needs such as hygiene, we get issued conduct rule infractions, the prison administration may confiscate the property items that we have become attached to, etc. In prison there is nothing you can do when these things happen. We just have to deal with it like everything else in here. Herein lies the problem. Why?

Many prisoners do not handle the above outlined problems in a healthy way. Sometimes they get violent with others out of frustration. Such destructive actions come with consequences. Therefore, most prisoners deal with their depression by sleeping. Like I said before when you are sleeping, you are dead to the world. In a state of sleep a prisoner does not have to deal with his problems. He can escape into his sleep. When he wakes up his problems are there staring at him in the face in the form of a four-wall cell or bars. To temporarily escape this existence, he falls back to sleep because it is too much to deal with right now. Therefore, he sleeps and sleeps some more.

Some people inside of these bars would sleep away all their years without waking up if possible. That is how dark of a place that prison can be within the human psyche. It is extremely difficult for many of us in here to face up to the mistakes we have made in life. The blame game is the biggest here. As long as a person is blaming someone else it allows him not to take responsibility for his actions. None of us prisoners are immune from this. It has its greatest effects upon those inmates who year after year keep on never ever wanting to take any responsibility, and this ultimately leads to depression. Again, to escape the depression people in here sleep more and more.

Another spectrum on this is when we get extremely bored in these cells. There is absolutely nothing to do sometimes but think. Too much thinking is not always good for you. It can drive you crazy in here if you are not thinking constructive thoughts. So how do you turn your mind off, of course you go to sleep. There you have it: sleep is the remedy in here.

The everyday ritual of monotony on doing the same things over and over again gets very boring in here. Men in here get tired of reading, tired of exercising, tired of watching television, etc. So, when a person gets tired of pacing the floor they just lay in the bed and think, and after they get tired of thinking about all of the things that they cannot change or have, then they do what comes naturally: they sleep.

In the above paragraphs I have painted a broad picture of the world of sleep and the lack thereof in prison. It is sad that nothing comes to a sleeper but a dream. Well, there is nothing wrong with dreaming. This world would be stuck in the dark ages without the inventors who dreamed up all the technological advances that we enjoy in society today. In prison sometimes it feels like we're stuck in the dark ages. Under the blanket wrestling with our depression, we get tired when the depression overpowers us and takes away our enthusiasm, therefore we get tired and drift off to sleep. Some wonder what measure of comfort do we get from sleeping? Ah, if you haven't figured it out yet then you will never know.

Okay, let me break it down further for you. When we sleep in here, we can dream. In our dreams we find all the actual things in real life that we are missing in here. In these dreams we are free, we are with women, life is wonderful. We go all over the place in these dreams, we go to parties, we fly away from here. This is partially why us prisoners sleep so much because it allows us to dream. Nothing is better to most of us in here than that. So, we sleep on.

Prisoners wake up in the foulest of moods. look at what they are waking up to. Do not disturb their sleep. No class of people gets more upset when you wake them up from their sleep than prisoners do. At times it is not because they are tired. Heck, they have been sleeping all day anyway. By waking them up you are disturbing something more precious than rest. You are cutting them off from their form of escapism to freedom and happiness. This is why sleep is sacred to these guys in here. When you have made so many grave mistakes to mess up your life and you are not doing anything to change it, you could get very depressed. In this state of depression, it is difficult to face all that you are dealing with. If on the other hand, you use this time to change your life, you will be active constantly doing things to uplift yourself and make something out of your life no matter how low you have fallen. In waging this internal battle against your depression, you are not trying to sleep all day. Your fight requires energy for you to be up putting the pieces of your life back together.

In a sense what I have said is that sleep can be your friend or your enemy in prison depending on your use of it. The proper use of sleep for the body is to give it its proper healthy amount of rest. To abuse sleep is to just sleep all day. For someone in the outside world not dealing with what prisoners deal with, it would be difficult to fathom why someone would spend so much time sleeping. It would also be difficult for a sober layman to understand why hustlers and addicts get so little sleep for nefarious purposes. In this brief chapter I have painted a clear enough picture for the reader to see inside our world inside prison, as well as to grasp a glimpse of the role that sleep plays in the dynamics of prison life.

THE ZOOZ
ZOOZ AND
WHAM WHAM
ECONOMY

Chapter 4
The Zoo Zoos
and Wam Wams

Economics in prison is a controlled underground black market. We call these items zoo zoos and wam wams. The penal authorities call it commissary or canteen. Technically it is market up items sold for five times their worth. Somehow the Department of Corrections justifies this. Such outrageous pricing automatically creates the need for a black market. Project Furthermore prisoners will hustle regardless of the reason. Such marked up prices on the canteen just creates an even greater vacuum and need for prisoners to hustle in here. In prison the Department of Corrections have their official canteen store and there are dozens of small stores inside each prison that the prisoners themselves commandeer. Everything that is sold in the prison canteen is also sold inside of the prisoners stores in their cells. Even appliances make their way back on to the black-market stores in here.

The economy in prison typically operates on what is called the two for one model. If one prisoner gives another prisoner one bag of chips, then the other prisoner must give him 2 bags of chips back and return when he goes to the official Department of Corrections canteen. If he misses a store day for whatever reason, then value increases, and he then owes 3 bags of chips or more until he eventually pays. A small debt such as that one can easily turn into almost a hundred dollars depending on how long the prisoner takes to pay his debt. The interest rates in here are higher than what the banks charge in the free world. There is a constant rush of traffic at these prisoner operated stores. If someone in here runs out of something he goes to the store man to get it until he is able to purchase it himself from the prison canteen. The only way to get around this is to have your own hustle, know a store man and so you can get things without paying any interest on it, or simply going without things.

Zoo-zooz and wam-wams (knick knacks and snacks) are nicknames for food items. Many of us do not know where these names derived from, but it is just prison lingo that we have used for years. Everything that you need is on the yard or in someone's cell even in solitary confinement. Satellite (mini stores) are everywhere throughout every prison. You have the most astute entrepreneurs in prison. People in here will find a way to survive and hustle. Believe it or not, prisoners who run stores save the day and prevent a lot of violence in here. If you do not have the items you need, how are you supposed to get it? A lot of men are in here for robbery. On the streets they took what they wanted. In this jungle prisoners think twice about going to rob the store man in here because he more than likely will try to retaliate. The store man go get robbed in here but usually it does not happen like that. If a prisoner needs some toothpaste to brush his teeth with and he does not have it, he goes to the store man to get it. The prison store keeps down a lot of commotion. When a prisoner owes a carton of cigarettes from a gambling debt and he has to pay it right now, he has to get that carton from a prisoner run store. If he did not get that carton from the prisoner store, then he would have gotten into a violent confrontation with whoever he was gambling with. They want their money today, not when he goes to the official Department of Corrections store that next week.

The penal authorities on paper officially banned prisoner run stores. They say it is illegal. However, the prison authorities turn a blind eye to these stores. They know that the prison run stores operate either way. However, they are also aware that these stores make their job easier because they keep down a lot of violence surrounding thefts among the inmates as well as debts. When a man is hungry in here and the meal that they're serving at the mess hall is something that he does not eat, then he will get the ingredients to make him a small meal from the prison store man. If a prisoner owes a debt, he will get it from the store man. Otherwise, depending on who he is or who he owes then this could cause a violent confrontation over the money. By the store man helping him to pay this debt then he prevents this possible explosive confrontation. A few dollars may seem small in the free world, but I have known prisoners to stab someone over it. They stab the person not necessarily because of the money, they stab him because of the perceived disrespect and the fact that if they do not deal with the situation then the other prisoners will think he is weak. When other prisoners sense this weakness, they will try to take something from the store man. One thing is for sure, that dudes in prison are very serious about their money, even if it is only one dollar.

You have guys in here serving life sentences with no chance of parole for killing someone on the streets for less than fifty dollars. So, what does he care about killing someone in here for a fifty dollar debt. Trouble is everywhere in prison and it is not difficult to get yourself in it. At least 30% of the prison population has some type of way they earn income in this prison economy. This keeps guys busy in here while at the same time giving them something to do in order to occupy their time. Some guys cut hair as their hustle, braid hair, others draw pictures, some fix appliances combo others exhort weaker prisoners, gamble, sell drugs, sell weapons or whatever to get by. Toilet paper, bleach, floor wax, or anything else is off for sale on the prison black market economy. These are some guy's hustle in here. Selling these household products from their prison job is how they eat. This is how the prison economy operates. When you live it, you understand it, while on the outside looking in, it all seems so petty.

Food from the prison kitchen gets stolen and sold on the yard. A lot of the street cooks and guards turn a blind eye to this also. Whatever food that the prisoners do not eat gets thrown away, so the prisoners have a way of getting it out of the kitchen. They sell these products as a way to survive. Some prisoners do not have anyone on the streets to send them money, so they survive off the prison black market economy. One guy may sell postage stamps half price. He has hundreds of stamps that he has gotten wholesale on the black market. Therefore, instead of going to the prison canteen to pay the entire price for a postage stamp, most prisoners just buy the stamps half price from the black market in prison from the stamp man.

Stamps

Postage stamps are the third most valuable staple in the prison economy. All prisoners need postage stamps to mail letters out. Stamps also get used as currency in here. You can purchase anything with stamps in here. Prison rules only allow each inmate to have so many canteen items due to lack of storage space etc. For example, the state of Missouri allows prisoners to keep 6 bags of chips, 6 boxes of cake snacks, 20 tobacco products, 12 meat products, 4 packs of batteries, 24 sodas, 24 soups, 100 postage stamps, etc. Everything has a certain limit that each prisoner is allowed to have. Of course, in here people find a way to circumvent all of these rules.

Nothing that I am saying is new in this book. Prison administrations have known these facts for over a century. They cannot stop it. Furthermore, they are aware that these stores help keep down a lot of violence that would otherwise be happening. Stamps can be hidden anywhere and prisoners who run sports gambling rings make several hundreds or even thousands of stamps each week. These postage stamps generate them hundreds of dollars. With this money is how many of them survive in here.

The stamp economy travels throughout the prison system. In confinement postage stamps are the soul economy. Prisoners who do not have money coming in from the streets will take a pack of cigarettes valued at five dollars on the streets, make fifty dollars from that same pack in solitary confinement. This precious cargo in here is worth twenty times its normal market value because of its exclusiveness. It is elaborately smuggled into solitary confinement. The prison authorities are aware of the ways that the prisoners smuggle it in.

Once they clamp down on one way of stopping it, the prisoners just get more creative while finding other means of getting it tobacco in. Tobacco is usually sold exclusively for only stamps and solitary confinement because the prison administration limits the canteen items that are purchased while on lockdown. We are allowed to purchase 100 stamps every store day. The vast majority of these stamps get used to buy tobacco by inmates who smoke. In turn these stamps come back out on the prison yard and get sold for half price. Since we cannot have paper money in here, postage stamps and cigarettes get used as paper currency. Of course, cigarettes are the most valuable staple in any prison economy. Prisoners crave nicotine just as they crave for freedom.

Cigarettes

Cigarettes are the main staple in the prison economy. You can buy anything and everything with cigarettes in here. They are like gold in prison. Ninety percent of the prison population smokes cigarettes. When a person does not have the funds to buy tobacco from the official Department of Corrections canteen, then he will go get these tobacco products from the prison store man. Some inmates smoke so many cigarettes in here that they use them as a substitute drug. Prison is a stressful place. Prisoners who smoke say that they smoke to ease their stress. Whenever the penal authorities tried to ban tobacco, they unwittingly create a black market. It then gets smuggled in through visits or the guards.

Top, burglar, or kite is the name that the manufacturer gives these tobacco products that are sold in prison. these tobacco products are cheaper than the name brand tobacco packs of cigarettes, so they get sold more in here. When a prisoner smuggles 20 bags of Top and takes it to solitary confinement (the hole), the prison lingo for that is called: making a Top Run. Actually, the guys in the hole are happy when the Top Runner comes because he brings that tobacco that everyone craves a smoke. It also keeps the stamp economy pumping as well. One Top roll of tobacco stick is worth 10 stamps in here. Stamps get traded, some posted stamps are sent to the street so family members can cash them in for money. The money travels and circulates far and wide and here. The prison economy squeezes super profits out of the most trivial products. Tobacco is the King product of the prison economy.

In prison we say zoo-zooz and wam-wams mainly talking about snack cakes and chips. Really though, zoo-zooz and wam-wams consist of the entire underground prison black market economy. Things in here are out of the open yet operating outside of the fringes. It may seem petty to citizens in the free world, but prison is an entire world onto itself. Prisoners are deadly serious about their money. A lot of our crimes were financially motivated, so the black market is brokered with intense passion in prison. This chapter is a short brief economic course on the prison zoo-zooz and wam-wams economy.

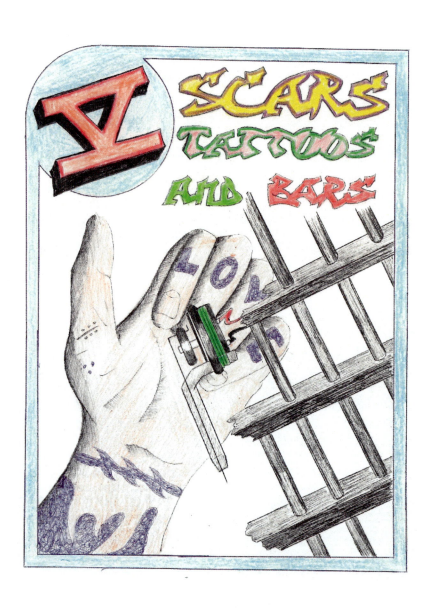

Chapter 5
Scars, Tattoos, and Bars

Scars are battle wound that many people in prison have. It is a blemish left behind from trouble in times past. It serves as a statement or mark of imperfection. Nothing is perfect about our life in prison. So, scars represent a reflection of the current state of our lives right now. A lot of prisoners have been shot or stabbed and as a exhibition to their war story they show off their war wounds. Guys actually brag about being shot or stabbed as if it marks the certification of them battled tested. The scars appear everywhere on people's body in here. Some of the scars are burn marks from fires, accidents, drug cooking explosions, or during escape attempts trying to get away from the policing while running.

Each scar has its own story. When you look at a person in here and see their scar and ask them how they got the scar, they have to tell you the story behind it. Some scars tell their own story. Dudes in here have been in a lot of battles in here and on the streets therefore there is a lot of scars in prison. That is a part of the prison story.

Tattoos are visual way to tell a story. A picture is painted to represent something. Prisoners were more tattoos than anywhere else in the world. Guys are addicted to getting inked in here. In prison lingo we call it getting tatted up. In such a bland place, guys expressed themselves with body art. Gangs are prevalent in prison, so guys put their gangs set or block on their body. The tattoos that people in here get are endless, but each tattoo means something significant to the person who gets it. Of course, you will see the craziest tattoos in the world on the body of prisoners. A few have their entire face tattooed. Others have their entire head tattooed. With nothing else to do guys in here will just make up reasons to get new tattoos.

Mentos to dead homies, family members, and tributes to their kids are the main tattoos that prisoners have. Tattoos of skulls are popular in here also. You can identify what a prisoner is about and where he is from through his tattoos. I do not have any tattoos, but mostly everyone in here around me does. A lot of dudes come to prison without tattoos, and they get them here just following trends. There is so many followers in prison. It may start off with one small tattoo of a teardrop under their eye. Then a small tattoo on their neck. Then they end up getting their whole arm tattooed, which is called a sleeve. After they get both sleeves done then they get their chest, arm, back and entire legs tattooed.

Walk through any prison yard on any given day you will see a lot of prisoners with tattoos. The ones with the most tattoos like to show off their body art. Their tattoos represent what they stand for. Tattoos are very cheap in prison. Plus, some of the best tattoo artists are in prison.

It is relatively easy to make a tattoo gun in prison. These guys in here are geniuses when it comes to devising machines to tattoo someone. Of course, people in here run a high risk of contracting diseases and infections through getting tattoos in here. To avoid that guys usually use new tattoo needles on every new person that they get tattoo on. Otherwise, infections can spread easily using the rudimentary tools the tattoo artist in prison use.

A guy can spend about an hour telling you what just ten of his tattoos mean. Each tattoo has its own story. That is why guys take great care in getting them. A tattoo tells the story of pain, struggle, sacrificed, triumph and defeat. Behind each shade and stroke is another layer of the struggle. Even beautiful artful tattoos can represent a painful episode or tragic loss. Other tattoos say what the guys feel towards the world. This may be explicit. Others just get tattoos for direction because they like the symbol or design. The prison authorities cannot stop the prisoners from getting tattoos. Tattoos are just a part of prison culture.

Bars

Bars in jail have a tremendous psychological effect upon a prisoner. The bars are like barbed wire which serves to remind the prisoner that he is locked up caged in. You have to look at the bars all day. It is like wearing a striped suit in jail. The bars make the statement that a man is barred from society. Looking at bars all day is a hell of a thing for the human mind. It is an image that stays with you. After so long a man behind bars can begin to feel like a caged animal. Why bars? What is the psychological purpose of the bars? Whatever the purpose may have originally been, the bars do have a hell of a psychological effect upon prisoners. In silence when he has to look at the bars it scars his mind. He feels trapped. For those who are locked up in prisons with bars I know how strong you have to be to go on with life although you are looking at bars all day every day stuck in a cell.

Bars, scars, and tattoos are a main part of prison culture and I have briefly talked about each of these elements as I paint a picture of the prison experience for the person on the outside (free world) looking in (inside prison).

Chapter 6
The Art of Storytelling

There are many griots in prison. Men in here have mastered the art of storytelling without being conscious of doing so. The majority of most of the men's time is spent telling stories or listening to stories being told. Some of these stories are true, some of them are false. The oral tradition of the story form captivates, but most importantly it entertains in a place like prison. Of course, we are always trying to pass time in here.

Prisoners are master storytellers. Each narrative is told with excitement and passion. Even sad stories are told in a way that takes you into the story allowing you to see the characters clearly and feel these feelings. We get caught up in the narrative here. The story form is how prisoners relive and recall their glory days. Prisoners love to live in the past because the past is all that some of us have or know.

As stories are being narrated, the prisoner's former life is painted on a vivid mental canvas for all of the listeners to join him past at the places where he was. We imagine how it was while picturing the scenery in our minds. We may have been in the same type of environment that he is talking about. As he tells the narrative, he mentally transports us into another realm of events. We mentally leave the prison and go to the landscape of the story. His tale paints a picture of his former life before he came to prison. Of course, some men will exaggerate their stories. The bragging is so heavy in here that you get used to it. As the guy is telling you the story from years ago, he happens to vividly remember what outfit he had on, down to the shoelaces. As he is putting all these colorful details in the narrative, the story last longer than a normal story would. Some stories are told for the exact purpose of bragging.

On any given prison yard, at any given time, you can find the majority of prisoners telling one story or another. Depending on how long a prisoner has been incarcerated determines the form of the story that he will narrate. The newer prisoners love to recite stories about the streets. A lot of the old timers tend to talk about penitentiary stories. They have been locked up so long that they begin to recite prison war stories.

War Stories

War stories are prisoners favorite form of storytelling. War is a battle, battle is exciting. Prisoners love excitement. The war story recalls danger, it gives you an adrenaline rush while you are telling the story or listening to it. This is especially so if you are a warrior yourself because you have been in these types of wars. Whether it is a shoot'em up Bang Bang or all out fist brawl, prisoners want to hear it. They get so animated in here as the war story is told. Their hands speak while flailing in the air to express themselves, eyes bulge, crooked smiles galore as the details are painted. In here firsthand accounts of a recent war story is like prime-time breaking news with the prisoner serving as the reporter. War stories travel in here so fast from one prison to the next. Especially the dudes who never have any static. They never have been in a war, but they love to gossip and so their day consists of gossiping about war stories they saw or heard about. They give about as good of a live report to the beholder's as they can give.

Some war stories maybe some work or dirt that the prisoner did on the streets. Warriors tend to revel in the stories. The more dangerous war stories he can tell heightens his warrior profile. In prison you hear a lot of war stories.

Cell Warriors

Some guys in here go to war behind a steel door. These guys are called cell warriors. He wages war with words and anything projectable of an object that he can find to throw from the cell. There are countless methods to the cell warrior's madness. First and foremost, he assails his enemy with fiery verbal threats or by a kite (a note written on a small piece of paper). He threatens to kill the other prisoner or guard. He calls them names. Then he proceeds to talk bad about their mother or any other relative of theirs whom he has or never will meet. He immerses himself in tales of the other persons misfortunes real or imagined. He says anything that he can hoping it will get under their skin. Afterwards he reverts back to threats of how he will kill them, etc.

The reason he is called a cell warrior is because he has no real intention of doing what he is threatening to do. Or he is just mad right now and will apologize to the other prisoner face to face later on down the line. Hence, he is a cell warrior because he only wars behind the door. Some cell warriors spend their entire prison sentence in solitary confinement. There is no possible way for him to carry out all these bogus threats that he is making. This guy probably will never see you again. Furthermore, cell warriors are notorious for doing this just to pass time. Threatening to kill and maim people is a form of recreational fun for them to pass time.

The cell warrior is always ready for battle. He wakes up out of his sleep and runs to the cell door in full battle regalia ready for war. If he hears the voice of his enemy in his sleep, he is alerted and proceeds to hurl verbal assaults in full offensive attack. Sometimes he just battles from his bed. These guys get so upset and hyped behind these doors. The battle seems all too real. A lot of it gets real serious. Sometimes these guys actually make good on their threat. Other times it is done for a pass time. Dudes who swear they would kill each other last week will become best buddies and team up against someone else who they are both battling with, inmates or guards.

Cell warriors do not bar none. They go to war with any and everybody. It doesn't make them any difference. As long as they have time to do, and a hundred-thousand-dollar door to stand behind, they can't be touched. So they battle on with whoever takes their challenge. You don't have to wrong them, just come into their zone and you become their target. Cell warriors are the kings of storytellers. Let them tell it, most of them have never lost a battle. In every war story that they tell they were the victor. Cell warriors proceed to tell war stories (or listen to them) all day, from the time they wake up until the time they go to sleep.

Even when a cell warrior is quiet, he is making preparations for his next war. If someone else is narrating a war story and he doesn't like it or believe them, then he starts threatening them and launches a verbal battle with them.

These cell battles rage on 24 hours a day and seven days a week. One guy screaming over the other. Banging on the door, kicking the door, etc., Just to be heard or to purposely wake the other prisoners up is the main war tactic of the cell warrior. He used other methods as well. There are too many to name here because the madness is endless. The other occurring tactics that the cell warrior uses are that he tries to prevent anything from going to and from his combatant's cell. He does this with string or whatever he can. He uses other underhanded strategies in his war chest as well. A lot of it is very petty. Instead of the prisoner doing something positive with his time, he wastes his energy and focuses on perfecting his cell wars. As long as prisons exist these cell wars will rage on.

In prison everyone has a story to tell. People without a voice long to be heard. What is the best way to be heard? Storytelling. Therefore, the prisoner becomes the greatest storyteller. We all have a past and in here being a prisoner is not something that most of us aspire to be. We had a life before we came here, and we will have a life after we leave here. All day prisoners recite their past history and tell about what they had before they came to prison. people talk about their former life because that is all that some of them have to look forward to because they are going back to that same lifestyle. Recounting their past as a reminder to them. They do not want to get lost in their prison life. Therefore, they give a continuous account of life out there. While we listen to their stories, we vicariously live through them.

The gift of storytelling is a blessing for all of us in prison. We need the form of storytelling in here. Not only does it help us to pass time, but it gives us hope and something to look forward to. For us prisoners who have been incarcerated for a long time these stories let us know what we have missed in society all these years we've been here. In a later chapter, I speak about the technology vacuum that we experience in here. Other prisoners always tell us about how it was for them using these technological gadgets and platforms.

Storytelling in prison is usually always done with flourish. When a prisoner first comes, he may only tell a story in a regular way. Soon though he catches on an learns that prisoners don't just tell stories in the normal way. The master storytellers recount their narratives with real life drama, excitement is thrown in, body language is distorted, the narrator is on edge, he is full of life. The story is told in a way that you must feel the emotion of the narrator. He does not have to holler but most important to him is that you feel what he is saying.

The art of storytelling is so proficient in prison that a prisoner will outline his biography for you in the form of dozens of very long stories that he tells you about his entire life from childhood to adulthood. The prison storyteller remembers what everyone wore on the day that the story took place.

He recalls how their voices sounded. He remembers the furniture in the house. He recalls the smallest details by recounting them with clear accuracy passionately.

As the story is being told, you wonder in amazement how does the prisoner's mind recall all of these small details. Sometimes you were there at the particular event that he is narrating about. You can verify what he is saying. It amazes you because you never remembered all of those small details until he bought them back to your memory. Prisoners have the sharpest memories. It is surprising because as he is telling the story you remember that you all were very high on this day. The prisoner may have been the highest person there, so how does he remember these things is what you wonder. When you are taken away from everything it is a form of nostalgia that we go through in here, and this nostalgia we recall even the smallest intimate details of people, places, and things because this is what we miss. In bringing back what we miss, we tell stories. To allow people into our former lives, we tell stories about the past. To recall an occasion that someone wants to know about, we tell a story. Stories are told about earlier that day, yesterday, etc. Prisoners use stories to narrate. Storytelling is our favorite form of communication in here. By using storytelling as a chosen way to communicate, prisoners have mastered the art of storytelling.

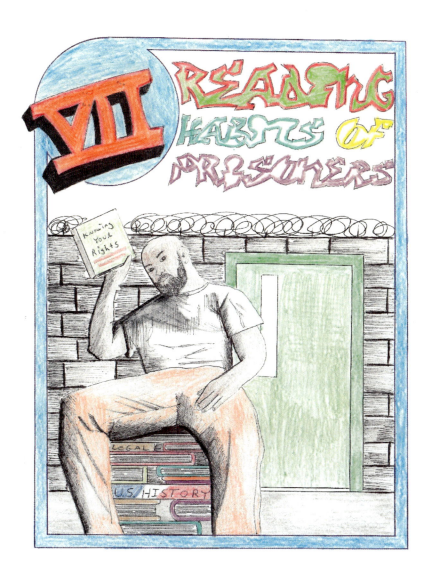

Chapter 7
The Reading Habits of Prisoners

Prisoners have the most serious of reading habits. Reading serves many purposes in here. Some do it to pass time while others take on prodigious studying habits that they will carry with them for the rest of their lives. Nobody can understand what reading does for us in these prison cells. As for me, reading makes me free. Books allow us to travel all over the world. Learning fulfills us in the most substantial way. The guidance that we derive from reading fills so many voids in our lives. Just reading the mystery, the story challenges our minds. Reading changes our lives for the better. Reading becomes like a natural high to us, getting high in a natural way. You can find peace in books, even in a chaotic environment such as prison.

Men in prison are hungry to learn because of how they starve themselves intellectually when they were on the streets. It is not like they are trying to make up for this, but rather they are just so intrigued with all of the new things that they are learning that it is difficult to get some of them to put the books down. When this new rich world of intellect is opened up to them it exposes their minds of visions that they have never envisioned before. Furthermore, books offer these men a form of escape. In such a limited prison environment, reading allows them limitless mental and emotional horizons to travel to. Imagine being trapped in a cell all day but reading allows your mind to go anywhere. Books become your companion. What you read in here becomes so intense.

You have different classes of readers in here. First, there are the serious studious readers who read some of everything in every genre. Secondly, you have the prestigious readers who only read the pastime. Even they learn a whole lot while getting their heart touched in the process. Thirdly, you have those who seldom read anything at all (reading only on the most needed basis). As for the first subset of readers described above, they are serious seekers of knowledge. They are searching for the deeper meaning in life. Reading is the only way for them to start reaching this destination. The more that they learn lets them know how little they really know. They begin to chase knowledge with the same passion that they chased money within the free world.

Exposure to these books awakens the humanity in these men. It puts them in touch with their moral side. Emotions are awakened that were buried long ago. This sets these men onto a different path in life. Reading is the great source of rehabilitation for these men. For those who are tired of the old life, books are the perfect vehicle for them to travel towards a different destination in life. There are different degrees to this, but once books get you into their hook you don't want to get away. You began to revel getting lost in the world of reading.

In the hectic environment of prison books become a sanctuary for us men in here. We find peace when we read. There is shelter and substance between the pages. This is where our hope is found. All we have are dreams in here, the things that we read confirmed that our dreams can come true. We seek success; what we read shows us that these accomplishments will not be easy, but nevertheless give us the blueprint on how to make it happen. When you read more and realize that there is so much that you do not know, it makes you aware that you have a lifetime of reading to do. We have time on our hands in prison, so if a person is a serious reader and here you will always find yourself reading something. Your mind becomes like a magnet to books, newspapers, magazines, and whatever else you could get your hands on to read.

The second class of readers who only read to pass time, mainly like to read a lot of fiction. They enjoy urban novels, romance books, science fiction, mystery, and fantasy of any type. They do not read for the literary value of these texts; their only purpose is to be entertained by getting lost in the story. This is their form of getting everything else off their mind. In here, dealing with so many different things keep so much on our minds. Reading gives us the space to relieve ourselves of this pressure. The reader in prison who only reads to pass time misses out on so much by depriving himself of the opportunity to really gain meaningful knowledge that will enable him to change his life.

The serious reader turns to books to educate themselves in various areas of life. Those who realize that they are lost turn to books to find themselves. This is accompanied by reading books of profound substance. A man must look within to find himself, but books show him which layers to pull back in order to do so. The search for meaning is a constant search, books serve as the map to show readers where they need to go. We get so much diverse material to read in here.

The timing of us reading a particular book coincides with the precise time that we needed to read that particular message. Sometimes it feels like a slight miracle to us. It is magical to our psyches. At first a person in here may start reading primarily out of boredom, but then it becomes a serious habit. People see us reading in here so much and they wonder why? As I have explained above, there are so many reasons that it is immeasurable. There are really no words to explain how good reading is to us and for us in prison.

The third class of prison readers are those who do not like to read it all. A lot of prisoners are this way. There are various reasons why they do not like to read. Ignorance is the number one reason. With all this time on their hands, many choose not to use this time educating themselves. Years path without reading books. There are those who choose to watch television all day and play games such as cards, Domino's, etc. They say that reading serves no purpose for them. They will only read something that they want to such as a letter or something. Reading as a habit is a foreign concept to them. Little do they know what they are missing without taking advantage of the many opportunities to reform their thinking which will allow them to obtain skills to survive legally in the free world.

A man that desires change in here can find a pathway for change inside of books. The more that he reads the more he sees how the world operates outside of the criminal circles that he limited himself to. Once he sees this, he then glimpses an opportunity of how he can fit into the world of citizenry living a meaningful lawful life. Books are so important in a place like this. Men in here who understand this become ferocious readers with an unquenchable appetite for knowledge. Knowledge changes their life while at the same time giving them a route to travel on a better path in life.

Reading gives us a way to express ourselves. The authors write stories that we can relate to. They write about things that we feel inside that we didn't know anyone else felt. Their words capture what we feel about the world. It is so captivating to us because we never knew the power of books like this before. When we were in the free world reading was the last thing on our mind as we were living the life of crime. Imagine someone who had for years limited himself to street crime now reading books on astronomy, philosophy, science, economics, history, etc. It makes us all appreciate life more. For real all this heavy reading blows our minds. We get lost in the reading. Discovering world upon world as you find us zealously reading one book after another. This is an experience that is difficult to capture in words. Nevertheless, I have attempted to give citizens of the free world a glimpse in here that is intellectually an insight into the reading habits of prisoners.

Chapter 8
Technology Vacuum

In prison, we experience a technology vacuum. I have been in prison for over twenty years, and I have never used the internet. I have never seen the internet. I have never used a cell phone. In here we read newspapers and magazines to tell us about the new inventions, but we cannot really grasp it. We also see countless television commercials that show us some of these new gadgets but that still gives us no real sense of how to physically touch these tools. All of the new terms boggle our minds. The average prisoner has no idea what software or hardware is. What is that? What is the virtual data cloud? How can you store data on a cloud? Where does this cloud exist at? In here we get stuck back in an old era. I have been incarcerated for over twenty years and the technology that was in use when I was out there is nearly obsolete.

The ways in which television is watched is different. The ways that cars are operated has changed. Everything is digital, but when I left the streets a lot of things were analog. I left the streets in 1995 when I was just 16 years old. The cars from when I left the streets are now called old school cars. Most phones still had cords on them back then. Everything has been upgraded. The cassette players that we had in our houses back then have vanished. VHS tapes have been perished. The clothes and music from when I was arrested is considered as a throwback now.

Due to security reasons, we are severely limited to the things that we can have access to in prison. We do not have access to the Internet. We cannot use cellular phones. The overwhelming majority of prisoners do not know how to use modern updated versions of computers. All of the media platforms keep changing every few years. What is popular now will fade away in a few years.

I have never physically touched a computer tablet, never saw an app, etc. Every year so many new gadgets are introduced into the technological field. New advances make three old brands seem outdated. Over the past 20 years or more I have not had access to any of these new things. There needs to be a balance somewhere. I understand his security measures must be put in place because of the serious crimes that many of us are imprisoned for. Surely society must be protected from any predatory behavior from prisoners in here. On the other hand, prisoners should not be banned or cut off from all of the technological advances going out in the free world.

Televisions were round when I left, now they are flat screens. Video conferencing, etc., were concepts that we did not imagine in the poor inner city ghetto neighborhoods where I grew up at. The majority of people in those neighborhoods did not have a personal computer in their homes. People have access to the entire world via the Internet right on their mobile phone. For prisoners such as myself, all I can do is imagine how it would be to operate these things.

After we are finally released, many of us will have to be taught how to operate these technological gadgets. Everything has passed us by. As I have said several times throughout this text, time waits for no man. Music is listened to on different platforms that keep reinventing themselves. Satellite radio, cable channels that we have never seen in here, podcast, etc., have passed by without us knowing the operational methods of these communication technologies. Technology keeps advancing on pace while we are stuck behind the walls in prison shut off from these technological advances.

Ironically despite this technology vacuum, there are many things in here that serve the purpose of violating serious prison infractions. The penal authorities consider themselves keeping security in place by not allowing prisoners access to modern technological gadgets, yet on the other hand they sell the product's out of canteen that we can make weapons with. It is understandable that there are certain special media channels that we should be kept from in here because of certain crimes that we have committed. However, we should not be cut off from everything when it comes to the many modern technological advances. There should be security mechanisms put in place where we have access to modern technological tools. As things stand now prisoners

are stuck in a technological vacuum.

Chapter 9
How Do You Be   A
Parent from Prison

It is very difficult being a parent while you are in prison, nevertheless, it has to be done. Just because someone comes to prison does not mean their parenting duties cease. The burden can become heavier in here. Prison impacts everyone in the prisoner's life, especially the children. More than half of the prison population has at least one child. There are more than five million children in the United states under the age of 18 years old who have at least one parent in prison. Research is outlining the fact that many of these children have increased risk of problems with academics, behavior, and later drug experimentation. Studies have shown that these children also have mental and physical health problems. Less than half of parents who are incarcerated get visits with their children. There have been hundreds of studies conducted that outline the impact on children who have a parent who is incarcerated. Statistics never tell the whole story. Studies in themselves can never tell the exact amount of psychological and emotional trauma that these children experienced while their parents are in jail. The system itself is indifferent to this epidemic. Yet it comes right in circle around when some of these troubled children kept committing crimes getting sent to prison adding to the already bloated overcrowded prison system.

I was a child of an incarcerated parent so I can tell you firsthand how it rips families apart when a parent is sent to prison. I am not unconscious of the fact that some of our crimes torn families apart through our violent senseless crimes. In this text I am just tersely covering the aspect of parenting from prison. I would briefly like to talk about how it feels to be a child whose parent is in prison. When I was twelve years old, my stepfather went to prison for drug dealing. He was sentenced to about seven years. This devastates our family. My stepfather Robert Brown had just married my mother prior to him being sent off to prison.

Although he dealt in drugs, he provided for her family as the breadwinner. He was a strong piece of the glue that kept things intact in our nuclear family. He was my mother's rock. He used to tell us about the pitfalls of his lifestyle. When the authorities arrested him, it was unbelievable to us. We were shocked. Not knowing the particulars of the criminal justice system, us kids somehow thought that he would come home the next day.

As the weeks dragged by without him, it emotionally devastated our family. His absence represented a big void that was there without him. Of course, life went on for us, but it was never the same without him. Emotionally it was painful without Robert Brown being there. It upended our world. We missed him bad. His phone calls from prison were the highlight of my mother's life at that time. She would light up and be giddy like a little girl when he called. They had a real love.

Us kids missed him also. Nevertheless, in our selfishness there were some things that we did not understand about adults, nor did we have any comprehension of what a prison marriage was like for our parents. Phone bills ran into several hundreds of dollars each month. It often got turned off due to the extremely high phone bills. My mother always found a way to get it back on in order to stay in touch with her husband.

Going to visit him was even more difficult for us kids. It hurts to see someone you love and a prison uniform and the fact that they cannot go with you when you leave as emotionally difficult for a child. We took that real hard. We were always used to seeing him in regular street clothes. He was sitting powerless in a prison uniform with guards having power over him watching his every move. As children we felt this was unfair.

Nobody took the kids emotions or mental state into consideration. We were affected the most by this, yet no one asked us how this would impact us. No social worker came by to get our input or opinion. No officer of the court asked us how his being sent to prison would affect us children. Why is this? Nobody explained anything to us although this series of events left us emotionally torn, confused, and loss. It crushed our childhood sentiments that he would be gone for years.

Kids wonder why the system would do this to their family. Why so many years? Our emotions were raw even months after he was sentenced. He was a part of our family that was taken away. Kids do not really take into consideration their parents' crime. It is difficult for them to separate their parents from their parents' crimes. Children do not see a criminal like the system does, all they see is their parent. The fact that they love them, miss them, and need them at home does not change. When our stepfather was sentenced, it left us children numb. The feeling cannot be explained. A piece of the child goes missing.

The reverse side of the equation begs to answer the question of how to someone be apparent from prison? Every person has to take their own individual experience in how they approach being a parent from prison. Here I will just cover this subject in general. Being a parent entails great responsibility. Being a mother is the hardest job in the world. Like I said before, when someone is arrested, they do not stop being a parent. In fact, the burden just increases because they are not physically present in the children's lives each day. Their children are ever present with them in their heart, mind, and soul.

The parents in prison need their kid's. presence also. They miss them terribly. It nearly kills them inside that they cannot physically be there to raise their kids. They long to be there to guide their children through the pitfalls that life takes them through. As a parent they feel guilty, so guilty about not being there for their child. All that is left for them to do is continue being the best parent that they can even be from a prison cell.

As a parent in prison, you are dealing with so much. First of all, you have to accept the pain that you have caused your kids due to your being absent from their life. You must take their emotions into consideration in your every interaction with them. Second, you must be very direct with them because indirectness will only alienate them more. They already feel alienated without you being physically present with them. In your directness you must display discipline with them. There are all kinds of issues to be dealt with. If you were not the parent on the streets, then this worsens the problem and heightens the drama.

If the parent was not always there and was neglectful of the child, this will create some tension, thus making it difficult for the parent to get the child's total respect. Gaining the child's respect is the most essential component of parenting from prison. Of course, love comes first, but the child must respect the parent in order to listen to the parents' advice. The problem of children not listening arises in a lot of prison parenting situations.

If the child follows the parent's instructions, then the parent feels as if at least they are reaching the child. Then they could tell their child about not repeating the mistakes that they made. The parent does not want to preach to the child. The best way is to teach by example, but it is hard to teach by example from a prison cell. It goes back to the old saying, "Do as I say, not as I do." parents in here must honestly explain their mistakes to their kids so that they can truly understand the consequences to such actions. By doing this a parent can paint a picture for them of where certain actions will eventually land them.

Each child is their own unique individual being. A letter is a prisoner's most valuable vehicle to reach out to their children. Through a letter a parent in prison can express their innermost feelings in deeper ways that they cannot face to face or over the phone. Our kids read these letters and feel what we say. Letters also allow kids to write and express their deepest feelings to their parents in prison. This allows parents to know what their child is thinking. This back-and-forth riding as part of parenting from prison.

Phone calls are a prisoner's lifeline to their kids out there. They talk to them most by telephone. The parent learns about what the child is doing at school, who their classmates are, etc. The parent asks the child what they ate today and gives them advice on better nutrition choices. Simply put, they try to do all the things that a parent in the free world does with limited means.

Of course, a parent in prison is limited from what they can do with their child. They cannot take them shopping, cannot take them out to certain activities, cannot go to their sporting events, cannot attend their school graduations, cannot tuck them in at night, etc. Imagine how the child feels going about these activities without their parent each day. It hurts and the void is there. They see their friends' parents at all of these events, but their parents will not be able to be there for years to come. nobody knows these kid's silent pain. Being in prison affects the kids more than it affects the parents who are in prison.

Visits are the only time that they have any kind of physical contact. Visits are so precious to both the prisoner and their visitor. A child does not like seeing their parent locked up, but they love seeing their parent. It is a compromise that they make for each other. Imagine the child's emotional state if they go through security checkpoint after checkpoint just to visit their parent. This is a controlled sterile environment no matter how it is dressed up. It is difficult for many children to be themselves in this kind of environment. All kinds of emotional tornadoes are spinning around inside of the child. These children never lose their love for their parents.

A child's love is innocently powerful, and the system cannot take that away. Their bond and love for their parents survives years of imprisonment. Something in the child refused to give up on their parent. No matter how many bad things that they hear about their parents, that does not change the love that the child feels for their parents. It is not spoken, it is felt. You can see this love in the child's eyes.

What about the parent? How does this look from their spectrum? For the parents, being able to see their child means the world to them. No visit is anticipated more than seeing their child. No bars or security checkpoint can dampen their spirits. They live for seeing their child. No feeling in the world can compare. The child is their hope. The child is the major factor in their longing for freedom. Connected by DNA, a bond that even the prison walls could not break.

No matter how big the child grows, the child will always be the parent's baby. So precious. The parent in prison gets giddy on the visits to see their child. They forget about prison and its cares for those moments with their children. Imagine how their hearts pound in their chest when they walk into the prison visiting room and see their child sitting there. It is the most precious sight to them.

Somehow it always seems like the child has grown a few inches since the last time that they saw their child. It always feels like this because the hours, seconds, and days prior to the visit were spent with the parent constantly thinking about their child directly or indirectly. Strong love.

In the child's absence the parent in prison worries constantly about their child. Their mind wonders what is their child doing at any given moment, what is their child eating? Is their child okay? Is there child misbehaving themselves? These thoughts are accompanied with anxiety, longing, love, worry, care, etc. The parent constantly misses their child.

Prior to the visit the parent will spend around two hours getting ready for the visit although they prepared for this visit all week or all month, which is prison time, slow time seems like forever with all of the emotion, anxiety, longing, and anticipation tied into the prison visit of parent and child. The parent will spend more than an hour grooming. They want to look great for their child. An observer would think that they groom themselves to look good for this visit. It is a date for the parent. They must look good for their child. They must be strong. They are still mommy or daddy even though they are currently in prison.

When the parent enters the visiting room and lays sight on their child, the world seems like a much better place. They instantly connect. The parent and the child both light up. It is such a beautiful thing. Anybody that witnesses this knows what I am talking about. Of course, it's sad to see them having to hug in a prison visiting room. Still, nothing can change their love, and this is obvious for all to see. They have each other and that is all that matters to them. When they are together, they tune out the world, they just try to focus on each other and the little amount of time they have to spend together. If there is more than one child, and the parent is talking to the other child, then the other kid will just stare at their parent while they are talking. From time to time the child's eyes scan the surrounding visiting room. The child is amazed at what they see. Who are all these people is what the child wonders? The child also sees dozens of other children visiting their parents in the visiting room. Seeing this lets the child know that they're not alone with their parent being in prison.

As the child continues to survey the prison visiting room, they cannot believe what they are seeing. How does their parent survive something like this with guards watching their every move? How do they deal with being around so many other prisoners? Their parents watched over their household when they were free but now their parents are being watched over by the guards. The child cringes at the thought of their parent being locked in a cell all day. To get their mind off such thoughts they talk to their parents to get lost in the moment spent with them when their parents seem happy.

Neither visitor wants an interruption, but time seems to fly by unbelievably fast during prison visits. No one wants the visits to come to an end. Even the stoic guards get touched watching the scene. Inevitably though the visit must end, this is a dreadful time for everyone when it is time to go. No one wants to depart. Again, the child is the one most affected. It hurts the parent as well, but they know they must be strong for their children as well as themselves. The majority of parents in prison know that they're counting down a few more years until they can finally join their children. There is a small minority of prisoners who will never be released. It is even harder for them visiting their children in prison. Nevertheless, no matter how much time they were sentenced to, they still must always be their child's parent.

When it is parting time, the child is crushed. They hate leaving their parents behind in such a place. As for the parent in prison, they are also torn they are happy and overjoyed about the visit, but it hurts them not to be able to leave with their child. Yet they know that they must return to their cellblock. Furthermore, they know that they must go on and continue with their prison sentence until they are released. They have to be strong. Their strength is their sanity. Thinking about their kids is what gets them through. Despite the circumstances they understand that they must try to be the best parent that they can be even from prison. As long as there is life in their body their parenting duties will continue. The parent still lays down the rules. They tell their child the rules and expects the children to follow the rules although they are not physically present with the child. The family dynamic comes into play then. As I pointed out throughout this text, the child is the most affected person when a parent is sent to prison. The child is the one who gets shifted around. When the parent goes to prison the child is passed along to an auntie, grandmother, or sibling to take care of the children while the parent is away. Therefore, the child must move into someone else's home and follow their rules. The child might have to switch schools. this entire process takes the kid out of their normal element. It forces them to get used to another surrounding. Some kids rebel against this, others began acting up or just completely get withdrawn.

The emotional trauma that a child actually experiences is way more dramatic than any study can put into words. The child realizes that life goes on, yet they feel absolutely sad that their parents are not here. Kids really dislike when someone else tries to tell them that they must also abide by whoever they live with and their rules. Oftentimes the kids complain to their parent in prison about the treatment they're getting, and the parent plays peacemaker. Sometimes they have to step in on behalf of their child, yet they also have to be balanced because they must be thankful for their sister, parent, or friend being there for their child and taking care of their children while they are in prison.

The part of the discussion that we have now entered centers around the financial strain that having a family member in prison places upon their entire family. A lot of times when the family members taken the children, they do not get financially compensated for this. It is very expensive to take care of children nowadays. Most of these caregivers already have children of their own to take care of. If they are already in financial straits, then taking in that extra child or children only adds on to their already dire financial situation. Usually this is the case for the average family. Still out of love for the family the child is taken in. We must not forget the millions of other children who are taken in by the state and given over to the foster care system. It will take an entire other book to write about what happens to these children once they're taken into foster care, etc. There are times when this actually helps a child when they are placed in an environment that is conducive to their proper upbringing.

I just want to briefly touch on how it is a great financial burden to everyone when a parent goes to prison. It is then left of someone else to financially take care of the child because the average parent cannot do so from a jail cell. The family struggles. The child must then relinquish some luxury's that they were accustomed to. They will have to downgrade. Taking the kids to visit their parent in prison can run into hundreds of dollars. Phone calls from prison are very expensive as well. Not to mention that the parent in prison also needs financial support to be able to purchase the things that they need in prison to survive. The list goes on, the financial strain placed upon the entire family is significant.

the parent in prison needs to be honest with the child about what is going on with the situation that they are in. Kids are much more mature nowadays. As the parent shares their real-life experiences with the child, it allows the child to learn. Being real with the child helps the entire situation. The child is already sharing in the parent's grief, so they may as well deal with what is really going on together. As such it helps them to better get through the situation that they're going through in one another's absence. The parent tries to stay out of trouble so that they can be able to talk to their kids on the phone and see them on visits. Therefore, they have to overlook a lot in prison. These are sacrifices that they keep on making for their kids even while they're in prison. Parental duties for them continue unabated. There is no break from being a parent, there is no vacation not even in prison.

Chapter 10
Pictures in Prison

Pictures are priceless inside jails and prisons. They hold the most weight in here than anywhere else in the world. Pictures tell us a story of what we are not there to see. Pictures are alive. They give us nostalgia, the memories seem so near. We live in the pictures and live through the pictures. The images stay imprinted on our minds for years. Sometimes in here pictures are the only way that we will see the past that we knew. It's all that we got. Years pass by in here without us seeing people that we love. Pictures are the only images that we will see of many of them for years to come. For instance, I have spent over two decades in prison. Many of my nephews and nieces were born since I have been in prison. They are now in college and I have never seen them face to face. The only way that I know how they look now is through pictures. For us in prison the pictures are so real. Pictures are like live motion pictures for us. It gives a real image to go along with people's voices. There are many family members that I have not seen in over 20 years except through pictures.

We hold on to pictures like they're gold in here. After a few years go by I get surprised by how much someone has grown or aged since the last photograph I have seen of them. Time only stops in prison, but it goes on so fast out in the free world. When we study a picture in here it can be like reading a lengthy essay. We observe every detail. The texture of the background takes on a back story in our mind. The pictures tell its own story. Not an inch of the photo will be overlooked by us in prison.

We survey the entire photograph. The eyes of the person in the picture tells us something. Their smile is a sign of life. Their jewelry is artifacts. A child smile represents an innocence that we never see in these cell blocks.

The parent in prison needs to be honest with the child about what is going on with the situation that they are in. Kids are much more mature nowadays. As the parent shares their real-life experiences with the child, it allows the child to learn. Being real with the child helps the entire situation. The child is already sharing in the parent's grief, so they may as well deal with what is really going on together. As such it helps them to better get through the situations that they're going through in one another's absence. This brief chapter has just outlined the things that go along with being a parent in prison. The parent tries to stay out of trouble so that they can be able to talk to their kids on the phone and see them on visit. Therefore, they have to overlook a lot in prison period these are sacrifices that they keep on making for their kids even while they are in prison period parental duties for them continue unabated. There is no break from being a parent, there is no vacation not even in prison.

A child in the picture represents the future. We wonder what is going on in their small minds. They have the entire world in front of them with so many opportunities to make good on their lives. What does it feel like to be a child? It seems that they are the only ones who know what true innocent fun is.

The glitz and glam of the picture show the layout better than a magazine cover. Even as I write these words right now, I am looking at pictures of my little brother's funeral from 10 years ago. Of course, I could not be there, but these photographs are my portal into that world. All I see is him lying in the casket looking at peace. Family surrounded him and it touches my heart. I am not physically there but I feel a part of the procession.

His funeral was more like a celebration of a short life. He died at 25 years old. These are my last images of him forever.

In many ways we get caught up in a time warp in here. So much changes daily out there. Images of the past are imprinted upon our mind. Prison attempts to disconnect humans from the world. Pictures serve as visual messages to us of the world we are missing. We interpose ourselves into the photographs because we know that if we were out there, we would have been right there with the people in the photograph.

When a parent is in prison, these are so valuable to them seeing their child. Getting these photographs is like sharing a moment with their child. Some parents are not able to visit their children due to the distance or lack of funds to pay for the visit. These photographs are the only visual they will get of their child for many years. When they get these pictures, they just stare at them for hours at a time. This is their only window into the physical world of their offspring. This is why pictures are priceless to individuals who are in prison.

At times, these pictures overwhelm us. When I look at my photo album, I see pictures of deceased loved ones. They are very much alive in my heart and I miss them. With these pictures they're still here with me. I am seeing how they were in the world. Their eyes are looking right back at me. The old saying goes: a picture is worth a thousand words. These pictures tell me stories that convey thousands of words and emotions. Pets in the picture are part of the family. Photographs do not get old in here. The image is as real today as when it was taken.

All we have is memories here, especially for those of us serving life sentences. All we possess of our freedom from the past is memories. Some of us tried to live vicariously through the past. Past memories are sacred in here. Via pictures, we build a shrine to the past. The present reality of prison life is harsh, so to cushion that hard reality, we soften it with pleasant memories of the past. Photographs are the perfect vehicle to preserve those memories.

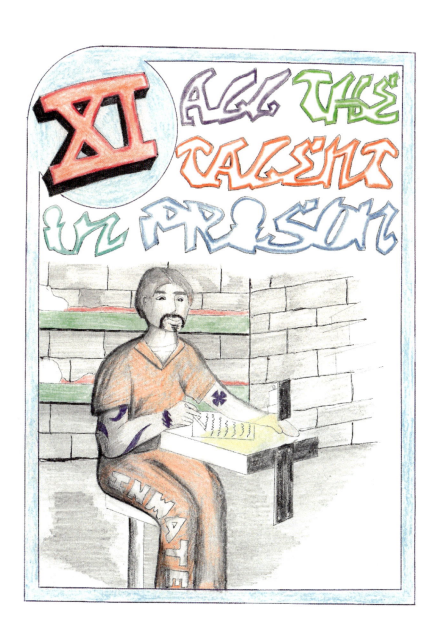

XI ALL THE TALENT IN PRISON

Chapter 11
All the Talent in Prison

There is so much talent in prison. Some of the brightest people do some of the dumbest things to end up here. The extraordinary talent that is inside of prison will simply amaze you. Some of the people locked in here are geniuses. When you see their skills up close, it makes you wonder why would such a talented person resort to committing crimes to get by when they could have made a living from their incredible talent? They could be using their gifts to help improve society. What a waste of talent by them languishing in prison. The art that these people in here create is unbelievably amazing. Their ideas are original, unique, and enlightening.

It is confusing that such intelligent men would end up locked away from society, when they are the ones who should have been out there contributing to society.

It is true that the system can lock up a person's body, but the system cannot lock up their mind. The brain is a place where they can create anything. They see solutions to the problems in society that people who are caught up in the problem cannot see.

The problem with all this talent is only when the criminal mentality sets in. The best of us are prone to it, but we must conquer such lower thoughts and replace it with a more constructive mindset. There are many scholars in prison. In every academic field there are people in here who have mastered it. There are scientists, architects, and every profession of every field inside these jails.

The main talent that people out there know about prisoners are in their drawings and writings. There is much more talent than that in prison. Some guys had already found their skill set on the streets before they misappropriated it to crime. Most prisoners like me only discovered our talent when we came to prison. With all this time on our hands, we were forced to look within and awake our sleeping genius. We had to find some meaningful purpose via a skill set we could take out into the world.

Since we are limited in our communication, and here we have so much to say. The pain and passion in our works are raw. The creations that men in here make are so intense. I do not know where all the talent in here comes from. I have sat in amazement and watched guys create something from scratch with raw materials. I asked them how they come up with that. When they explain their creative process, it leaves you dumbfounded. Some guys know how to fix just about anything, especially electronics. They come up with methods that no one else would think of.

Years get invested into their talents. To those in here that are on a true progressive path towards change, they give their skill set all of their effort. If some of these men were placed at the table at the United Nations, they could propose reasonable proposals to lead us to World Peace. To prevent a lot of the violence that would otherwise happen in here, men must learn to be the best negotiators. It is not just money on the line, it is people's lives.

As I have said before in another book about prisoners, "Life Goes on Inside Prison," that life does not stop for them once they come to prison. Life goes on for them. With time on their hands, they have much space to allow their talents to blossom. Guys that come here and teach themselves to draw and tattoo end up being among the best in their field. Their art leaves viewers in awe. These men actually create masterpieces. A lot of barbers are self-taught in here. Academic professionals in here are self-taught. The list is endless.

The creativity that blooms from these prison cells is wonderful. Prisoners have amazing gifts. They have a propensity for learning. With this learning they bring out their genius. They discover their own full potential which has been lying dormant for years while they were out there committing crimes. This is why when they finally come into one with their talent it makes such a phenomenal display. Some of the world's greatest minds are in prison.

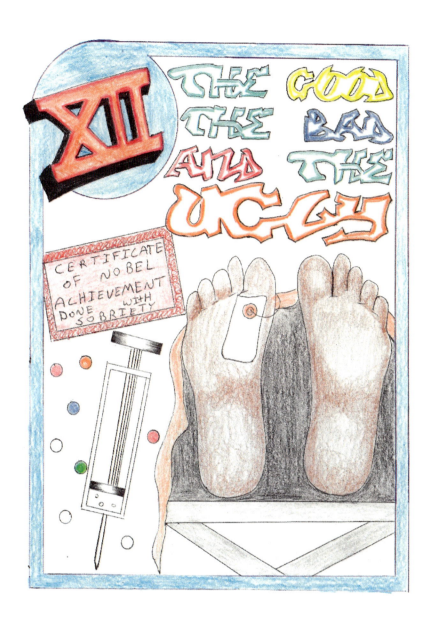

Chapter 12
The Good, Bad, and Ugly

There are good things about prison, and I want to briefly talk about these things. As sad as it is, some of us needed to come to prison. We would have never found ourselves, nor became the men we needed to become living the criminal lifestyles that we were living. We had to become sober. We had to have everything taken away from us so we could look deep within ourselves in order to find a deeper purpose for life. It has been right here in these prison cells that we discovered our humanity, thereby becoming reformed human beings. Going through the worst experience in our lives has taught us to bring out the best in ourselves. Contrary to popular stereotypes that is given about prisons, I can honestly say that there are some good men in prison. this is especially for those who have changed their lives for the better. They will do whatever they can to help others.

The good thing about prison is when a man uses time to read, study, and learn true life lessons. When people really rehabilitate themselves, prison then becomes a good thing for them. If you look throughout history, it was men who have been to prison who changed the course of the world. A lot of good does come out of prison despite all of the bad.

The Bad

Of course, there are a lot of bad things that go on in prison. Among the criminal elements, a lot of bad things happen. There are some bad people in here. All of us who are guilty of our crimes did bad things to get here. Many terrible things happen here. I have outlined some of it here and in my other text about prison life. Some of the things that go on here are outright violent, senseless, and petty. Wars get started over a pack of cigarettes almost daily somewhere in some American prison. We have all went to war about someone looking at us the wrong way or saying the wrong thing to us in here. This is a jungle. You have to stand up to all challenges or become their prey. On the streets you could walk away, but in prison when you walk away you look weak and walk into more problems. So, you have to stand up in here. That is why so much violence goes on in here. The negativity is a real bad thing. The system overall has many bad things about it. This text is not meant to be a grievance so I will not launch into a harangue about all of the bad things that go on in prison.

The Ugly

The ugly in prison is about as ugly as it can get. Downright evil goes on in here. The worst of men have been convicted of doing the most evil things. A lot of guys are never going home. They are full of hate and misery with nothing to lose but a life spent forever behind bars. Violence is the language that speaks the best in prison period extreme violence is what they understand here. The most ugly thing about prison is negative attitudes from the guards as well as the inmates which leads to more violence. Nothing is a pretty picture. I have tried to paint a fair and truthful picture about a place that I have languished in for more than twenty years.

Laughing To Keep From Crying

Prison can be a very serious place, but oftentimes it is just the opposite. Nowadays it is not like it used to be. When I first came to these maximum-security. prisons, everyone had a lot of time and walked around like they were carrying the world on their shoulders. Dudes have rough looks, permanent frowns, deadly scowls, and sinister smiles. The tension in the air was always thick. I have spent years studying how things have changed in here. I wondered why so much has changed, and I have slowly figured it out. It seems like a lot of these dudes play all day. Spending years in here is a sad existence. In the past decades, we dealt with everything real serious and doing time was serious. The seriousness of the predicament was too much for dudes to handle so they started playing and jesting as the order of the day to pass the time.

Some dudes play all day. What is funny about spending years in prison? Nothing. They make a game out of the serious things in life and make the games like they're serious things. I guess they feel like if you stay stressed out and angry all of the time about prison life, it will drive you insane. Playing eases their minds. In other words, they laugh to keep from crying. When you play, you are worry free. There are many games played in prison. There are cards, sports, gambling, playing the freaks, play fighting, cracking jokes, shuckling, living, and just plain old jesting.

Nowadays a lot of these guys play with each other as well as play with guards all day. Dudes wake up playing in here. They do not take their time serious nor take life seriously. This plays a part in the high rate of recidivism. If more people in here would take a serious look at their predicament in life, then they would take it very hard. They do not want to deal with harsh reality head on, so play becomes a mechanism to avoid being stressed out as a guy is not using his time constructively to change his life.

As I bring this text to a close, I hope that I have been able to give the free citizen an idea of how time in life in prison goes. There is a lot of good in here also period of course there is more bad, but the person who seeks more out of life has to weigh it all out and get the good that he or she can get and this hard situation. Society must know what goes on in its prisons. That is why I have documented this record for free citizens to see what goes on in here. This is a firsthand account from a young man who came to jail at 16 years old and has spent over 25 straight years in here in numerous maximum-security prisons. I have given the readers an account of the endless moments of

time spent in prison with the good, bad, and ugly.

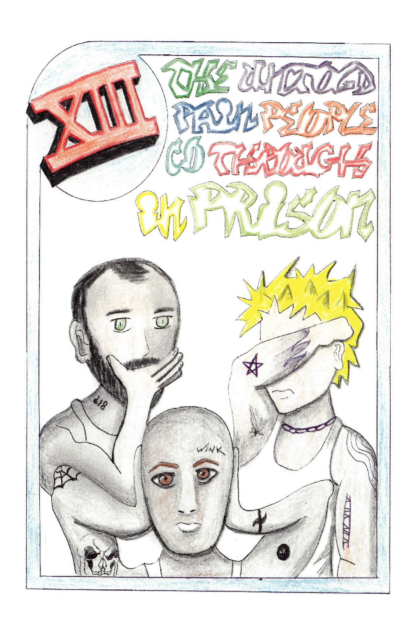

Chapter 13
The Untold Pain People
Go Through in Prison

The unnecessary pain that human beings experience behind prison walls is shocking. A lot of the suffering goes untold or is left unspoken countless civil suits are worn by prisoners who are intelligent enough to Sue for the blatant violation of their clearly established constitutional rights (see back issues of the award-winning magazine Prison Legal News and its website www.prisonlegalnews.org). But what about the 10s of thousands of other prisoners who never file a suit about their injustices. The list of atrocities being suffered every day is endless. I am not just writing about it as a bystander, I am living it every day and I have done so for over a quarter of a century.

No one is suggesting that prisons should be a cakewalk. People have committed serious crimes against society that landed him in prison. Nevertheless, they are still human beings and deserve to be treated as such. However, some guards known as correctional officers, look at prisoners as people who should be punished throughout their entire period of incarceration. With the years that they've been sentenced to alone is a heavy burden that prisoners have to carry. However, prison by its various design will make them suffer. A man or woman will suffer the regret of the many mistakes that bought them here. It hurts knowing the countless things that you are missing out on during the many years you've spent in prison. As I've said before, it is not so much as the physical pain as it is the emotional and soul pain you experience inside of prison.

Writing about this pain is raw pain. It starts the minute that the handcuffs rip into your flesh. As I write this, I would be amiss to neglect to mention the pain that as prisoners have caused to our victims. We caused pain to their body, minds, and spirits as well. So yes, we deserve to suffer for our mistakes too. I know that some pain never ends. but there does come a time where we should all seek to find a healing or else allow the pain and grief to overwhelm us. And in writing this, I don't mean to overlook the pain of our victims. I am so sorry for all the pain that us prisoners have caused our victims.

I do not intend to be insensitive to the ongoing pain being experienced by the victims of prisoner's crimes. Here in this book, I am just writing about the pain that people in prison experience on a day-to-day basis. In doing so the moment that the handcuffs are put on you sends you into a notion of a reality of captivity. The freedom that you knew before is restricted period from entering new jail cells and prisons you are constantly being processed. You only have control over your thoughts and actions. Your every move is being monitored by someone. It seems that even the things that you get away with in here come back to haunt you. What people call "karma" is in full effect inside of prison. Couple that with "Murphy's Law" and you begin to see the picture.

Another certain rule in prison is that if something can go wrong, it will go wrong. That is a constant truth within prison walls. The old saying goes, "if it isn't broke then don't try fixing it" gets turned on its head in the penal system. The prison authorities do the exact opposite thing. When things are going smooth, the prison authorities like to shake things up. This in turn makes it harder for prisoners to do their time in ways they've grown accustomed to. Therefore, they tend to suffer more and more. As you get processed in an out of different jails, countless changes take place. you have no choice but to adapt. Or as one would say "sink or swim." In prison you swim with the sharks, so you have your shark teeth to defend yourself at any given moment. Violence in here is ceaseless. Of course, the wolves are restless. Everybody wants to be fed. The problem is that they are feeding themselves with the wrong things. Therefore, the pain gets deeper.

What you knew before in the free world is gone. Pain sets in the moment you step in here. The pain of being away from your loved ones, the pain of your mistakes, the pain of a cold lonely cell, man the pain can be endless; just like the time of endless moments spent in prison. Imagine the pain of a mother who can't raise her kids because she is in jail; a father who can't protect his daughters from predators because he sits in prison. Prison hurts in untold waves. It hurts in ways that no writer can truly explain. It is something that must be lived to know it. The writer in this instance can only give you a draft of what it is like inside prison. But I want the reader to walk on this journey with us, and I hope that this book has allowed you to do so.

Just to give you another example of how pain comes in many forms in here, let me give you a portrait of the day of my 25th year in prison. It was during the winter season. On this day, I was stuck in a solitary confinement cell. The air was blowing so hard that it was bone freezing cold in the entire building that houses the hole, which is administrative segregation. I was only given a t-shirt and pants with a thin blanket. Icicles were on the window of the cell. Freezing air blew through the windowsill. The only way to keep relatively warm is to stay under the blanket. At night you shiver from the cold between the few hours of sleep you managed to sneak in. A few days later, I was moved to an in cell which is 5 times colder than the cell I was in previously. I declared my cellmate as an enemy which was the only way to leave the cell. As a punishment and retribution, I was made to sit on a small iron bench with leg shackles on while my handcuffs were shackled to the bench behind my back. I sat in his painful position for over 3 hours. Expecting relief when I was told I would move to another cell, I was met with more retribution. The prison authorities decided to teach me a lesson by placing me in another end cell that was freezing. This is how they make you suffer in here. As they escorted me handcuffs to that cell, we got there only to find it flooded and was inhabitable. A shocked guard then escorted me to the cell next to that one where the air was blowing freezing cold air at an exceedingly high rate. I know that sometimes prisoners exaggerate, but this is no exaggeration. I laid in that cell for approximately 20 hours and then I was released from solitary confinement after a week and moved back to a general population cell. These cells are about 40 degrees warmer. The ventilation systems actually blow out heat. Plus, we can bundle up in our own purchased winter clothing. You have your own television, radio, access to the phone, showers, etc. This is the difference between solitary confinement and general population. Solitary confinement only triples your pain in prison. That is what it is designed for. Vindictive guards can make it even worse. While all of this is going on, prisoners are at a constant war with each other period hurt prisoners hurt other prisoners. This is an endless cycle.

On top of all the internal and external pain that they are already experiencing, prisoners stay engaged with combat against each other for whatever disrespect or perceived wrong a prisoner did to them. In here there are just some things you can't let go or turn a blind eye to. Again, someone strikes with a fist, knife, or impoverished weapons. We are all caught up in it. The pattern repeats itself. We all suffer. Some go to solitary confinement, some face prosecution and get years added onto their sentence. The prison goes on lockdown for days on end. There is nothing to do but read, write, watch television, exercise, or other small things you can do in a small 6 by 9-foot cell. Let me tell you about prison. I am writing these words while on lockdown during a custody count.

Custody counts often get screwed up. People in here always say that the guards are too stupid to even get count right. Other times it seems like the guards intentionally screw up the custody count. Until count clears, nothing moves in the prison. So, to be vindictive to us prisoners, a lot of prisoners assume the guards do this on purpose so we can be locked in cells longer, which means less work for the guards.

Mind Games

The mind games that are played in prison is mind boggling. The guards try to catch prisoners doing wrong and prisoners try to get away. A lot of it is petty. There are endless rules that prisoners must follow in here. The prison administrative can use that to their advantage to keep their authority in control. Other guards misuse their power and use mind games as a mind control tool. Nevertheless, it can't all be blamed on the prison administration or the guards. As I pointed out throughout this book, the biggest of all mind game players is the prisoners themselves. When it comes to prisoners playing mind games against the prison staff, their success only lasts so long. The odds are against the prisoners. The guards have figured a lot of this stuff out after decades of observation. Sometimes to keep things smoothly, they will play the mind game along with the prisoners. The prison staffs main concern is safety and security. If it takes some playing into the prison politics to get this done, then they will use it to their advantage.

Why do prisoners play mind games amongst each other? I have asked myself this question a thousand times. It is hard to come up with an exact answer to this madness but let me give you a few answers that I have arrived at. The first reason I would say that they play mind games is out of boredom. On the streets people say, "there is not enough time in a day to get everything done." In prison we say, "there is too much time in the day with nothing to do." That is why I wrote this book with the theme of "time." time means a lot of different things to a lot of different people. In this book, I have outlined what time means for people in prison. To learn more about this, read my other book "Life Goes on Inside Prison" and other writings by me.

Does the mind play games on you when you have too much time on your hands and nothing meaningful to do with it? The majority of prisoners will answer yes to this question. When a prisoner's mind starts to play games with him or her, then he or she will start to play mind games with others; especially those locked in prison with them. It starts with the most pettiest of things. A miserable prisoner becomes an expert at playing mind games. They hate to see prisoners enjoying any peace of mind that they can't attain for themselves. So, they play mind games to disturb their peace. These mind games can consist of making noise when other prisoners are trying to read or sleep. It entails just getting in their way as well as distracting them in any way possible; gossiping, playing games, etc., the list is endless. People in prison stoop to the lowest of low levels.

Prison politics can accelerate to an all-time high. Whatever low senseless vile thing that can be imagined, is the extent that mind games are played inside of these prison cells. That's all the details that I need to give on that. Some bored miserable prisoners spend the majority of their day playing mind games. Too many times to count, I have reacted to these petty small-minded prisoners and ended up fighting or arguing with them or worse. In time, a progressive minded prisoner must learn to overlook these mind games. The reason why is because mind games will never cease to be played in prison. It all goes back to the untold pain I am writing about. Instead of allowing the pain to drive them insane, prisoners find the smallest things to do with their minds. On the other hand, progressive prisoners try to heal from the pain that they experienced. They do not allow the pain to overcome them, they learn to overcome the pain. That's the ultimate struggle in prison.

Pain will always be a part of this experience. Most of the times people in institutions feel helpless and powerless to do anything about it. And turn they turn to the pain in on themselves. This only makes the pain worse while causing it to intensify. Others take their pain out on other people. In this brief chapter I have only touched the surface of the pain that people inside of prison endure. Yet no book about prison would be whole without talking about this pain that is at the surface of the revolving door of prison. Yet this pain goes untold or is left unspoken. As I pointed out at the beginning of this chapter, a lot of this pain is unnecessarily inflicted on prisoners by the guards as well as by the prisoners themselves. This pain causes the endless moments in prison to stretch out even longer. Prisoners must learn to rise to the challenge and find purpose in their pain.

The Human Being Behind the Prison Number

Once a person is convicted of a crime and sent to prison, they are automatically assigned a prison identification number. For all intents and purposes, in the eyes of the system, the person then becomes a number. In order to receive their mail, commissary, or even dial an outside phone number, they must state their prison identification number. Furthermore, in order for them to walk out of the prison door as a free citizen they must state their prison identification number to the guard who processes people in and out.

Nevertheless, we must ask ourselves who was this person before they became a prisoner. Surely, he/she is someone's father, brother, sister, mother, aunt-tee, uncle, or cousin. A person doesn't lose their humanity by being branded with a prison number. With millions of prisoners in their custody, the state and federal government is a bloated bureaucracy that doesn't have the capacity to address the individual needs of its prisoners. In such an overpopulated and benign system, it is much easier to assign each human being a prison number. By assigning the person a number, it is much easier to look at them as a thing.

Prison is a well-oiled machine. Just because a machine is well oiled, doesn't mean that it runs well. In fact, the prison machine is broken in many places. Whenever the prison machine is found to be broken, it is clear from the prognosis that the entire machine needs to be fixed. However, the status quo has no vision or appetite for such. Therefore, the broken parts just get taped or welded back together to function temporarily and the broken prison system just keeps on churning. You can tell that a machine is broken from the products that it manufactures. Prisons are named as correctional and rehabilitation centers. However, their customer satisfaction rate is very dismal because they produce a 68% recidivism rate.

What becomes of people when they are sent to prison? How are they treated? If you ask the majority of prisoners, they will tell you that the system treats them more like a wheel in a clog, than as the human being that they consider themselves to be. This is where incarceration becomes a lose-lose situation for the state as well as the people that it incarcerates. No one is suggesting that prison should be a nice or even a pleasant place. Most people have done some bad things to end up in prison, but does this mean that society should treat them bad? These same people will one day be released into the surrounding communities that imprison them. Society needs to truly attempt to rehabilitate these men/women.

A person will always be more than a number. Guards (i.e. Correctional Officers) who abuse their authority treat prisoners as something less than human. It's true that some prisoners have done some inhumane things in society, but they are still human. In order to rehabilitate them, we must find and bring out their humanity. Remember they are someone's family member. He/she had a life as well as an occupation prior to coming to prison. Let's give them the respect that they deserve as human beings. Let's find out where they went wrong. How as we as a society help them to correct the thinking errors that caused them to commit crimes? How can we show them a better way? We must strategize on demonstrating to them that getting high off of drugs will not solve the problems they are experiencing. Illicit drug use and the securing of funds to support their drug addictions will only lead to the commission of more crimes.

The majority of crime has its root directly or indirectly tied to drug use. Who were these prisoners before they became drug addicts? Let us look at them in the shadow of this light instead of seeing them only as a zombie of their old selves. It becomes easy to dehumanize a drug addict if you didn't know that person before they became their worse selves. Then when the addict becomes a prisoner, it makes it even easier for a person to view them as less than. When society places prison guards with this incorrect mind frame in positions of authority over these people, it becomes clear how they can feel less guilty of treating them as only numbers and not as a human. Overworked and underpaid only adds on to the frustration of guards who feel as if the state doesn't appreciate their contributions. Some guards feel as if it is their moral duty to give prisoners a hard time. When prisoners are mistreated, this heightens tensions. Must we not forget that prisoners are human beings too? They are someone's mother, sister, father, or brother. If we can see them in this light, we will treat them better. As humans they will no longer be looked upon as a number or a thing. Once we see their humanity, then their prisoner identification number is only an identifier, just as a fellow guard and his/her fellow co-workers have an employee identification number. When prisoners are treated in a humane way, it tends to make them want to become better. In turn, they seek the help that they need to correct the errors in their thinking. Once these men/women truly seek to rehabilitate themselves, then it becomes a win-win for everybody. As society and the world at large, we must see the human being behind the prison number.

About the Author

Bobby went to prison at 16 years old and has lived inside prison walls for over 25 years. During his time of incarceration, he has obtained an Associate of Science degree and currently working towards a bachelor's degree in Sociology. Having lived through actual experiences of the school-to-prison pipeline and other ills that affect prisoners, makes the author able to use his actual experiences to academically talk about prison life. Not using fancy language or confusing psychological terms, the author just talks about everyday bare bone facts from someone who is living it and not just academically talking about it. This allows the readers to relate on a deeper level and feel what has been written. With this, the author thanks everyone who has taken the time to read these words in this book. Sincerely.

Afterword

I hope that this book has enlightened readers to the many facets that exist inside of prison life. As I've said before "Life Goes on Inside Prison." We who live it or have lived it, need to tell our fellow citizens about our experiences inside of those living tombs. People are curious to know what goes on inside of prison walls. I hope that this book has aided them in this quest. Television doesn't capture the full picture of prison living. People need to know what happens on an emotional, spiritual, and mental level in jails and prisons. This book has met that task. No one expert can claim to have all the answers in this field. All of the experts in every discipline need to connect with the prisoners themselves to find the answers. The best experts are the prisoners themselves who live the struggle of life inside prison.

Other Books by Bobby Bostic

Dear Mama: The Life

and Struggles of a

Single Mother

Generation

Misunderstood:

Generation Next

Mind Diamonds:

Shining on Your Mind

Mental Jewelry:

Wear It on Your Brain

When Life Gives You

lemons:

Make Lemonade

Life Goes on Inside

Prison

Also look for future books, products, and merchandise by Bobby Bostic.

Made in the USA
Las Vegas, NV
30 December 2021